MY FIRST BOOK OF
MAMMALS

WRITTEN BY ELIZA JEFFERY

ILLUSTRATED BY OLGA KONSTANTYNOVSKA

CONTENTS

Words in BOLD can be found in the glossary.

WHAT ARE MAMMALS?

Mammals are AMAZING!

You can find mammals in the sea, on land and even in the sky! A mammal is an animal that has these four things:

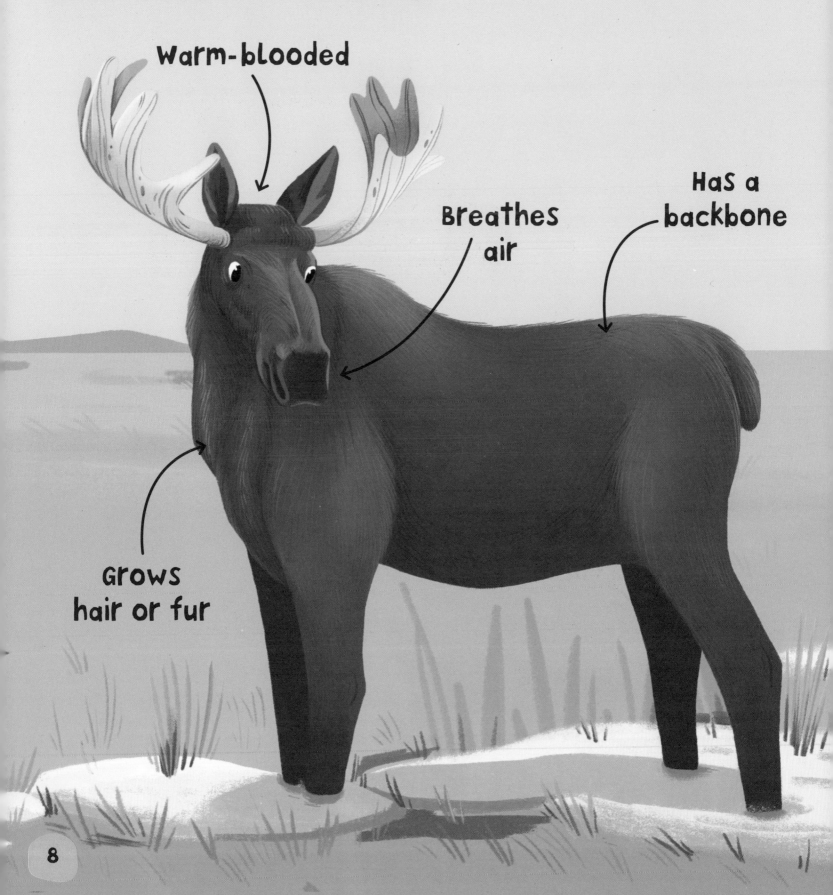

Warm-blooded

Breathes air

Has a backbone

Grows hair or fur

Mammals' young

All female mammals produce milk to feed their babies.

Keeping warm

All mammals are warm-blooded and so can live in places that are very hot or very cold!

Types of mammals

Most mammals have four limbs, apart from animals like whales and dolphins. Humans are a type of mammal too!

POLAR BEAR

Polar bears are the LARGEST CARNIVORES on land!

These wild animals are clever **predators**. They like to hunt on sea ice, waiting for seals to appear at the surface of the water, before pouncing!

Excellent sense of smell

Mothers and cubs have strong bonds.

They stay safe in snow dens.

DID YOU KNOW?

I am a... **carnivore.**

I eat... seals and fish.

My babies are called... cubs.

I can be found... in the Arctic.

SHREW

Shrews are the SMALLEST MAMMALS!

They are similar to mice in shape, but shrews have long, pointy snouts and usually live outdoors. They eat every 3-4 hours to stay warm and full of energy.

Sharp claws for climbing

Razor-sharp teeth to catch **prey**

Good sense of hearing, smell and touch

DID YOU KNOW?

I am an... **omnivore**.

I eat... insects, seeds and **fungi**.

My babies are called... shrewlets.

I can be found... everywhere, in hedgerows and woodlands.

Shrewlets huddle together for warmth

GIRAFFE

Giraffes are the TALLEST MAMMALS!

Giraffes are most well known for their long necks. They are peaceful animals that spend most of their time **grazing**. They live in groups called corps or towers.

Every giraffe has a different patterned coat.

They are always standing up, even when they're sleeping!

14

Long tongue to grab branches

DID YOU KNOW?

I am a... **herbivore**.

I eat... leaves, twigs and fruit.

My babies are called... calves.

I can be found... in Africa.

WOLF

Wolves are the LARGEST members of the dog family!

Wolves live in groups called packs. They work together to hunt and survive, with each wolf having a different job within the pack. Wolves often spend hours tracking down their prey.

Thick coat for warmth in colder months

They communicate by howling.

DID YOU KNOW?

I am a... carnivore.

I eat... deer, moose and wild boar.

My babies are called... pups.

I can be found... in North America, Europe, Asia and Africa.

Super sense of smell for tracking prey

BLUE WHALE

Whales are the BIGGEST MAMMALS in the world!

Blue whales can be as long as three school buses! They have smooth, rubbery skin and slender bodies for gliding through the water. They come up to the surface to breathe air.

Barnacles hitchhike on whales' bodies.

18

Blowhole to breathe air

Flippers and tail for steering

DID YOU KNOW?

I am a... carnivore.

I eat... krill, plankton and other mammals!

My babies are called... calves.

I can be found... in every ocean, except the Arctic.

19

LION

Lions are STRONG and have a POWERFUL ROAR!

A lion is one of the biggest cats in the world. Males are in charge of looking after the cubs while females are out hunting for prey. Newborn cubs have light spots on their fur.

A lion's roar can be heard up to 5 miles (8 km) away!

Male lions have a thick, bushy mane.

A group of lions is called a pride.

DID YOU KNOW?

I am a... carnivore.

I eat... large animals, like zebra and wildebeest.

My babies are called... cubs.

I can be found... in Africa.

PLATYPUS

Platypuses are the only mammals that LAY EGGS!

Platypuses hunt underwater and can spend up to 12 hours each day searching for food! They are very shy animals that usually live alone.

Male platypuses are **venomous.**

Webbed feet help with steering underwater.

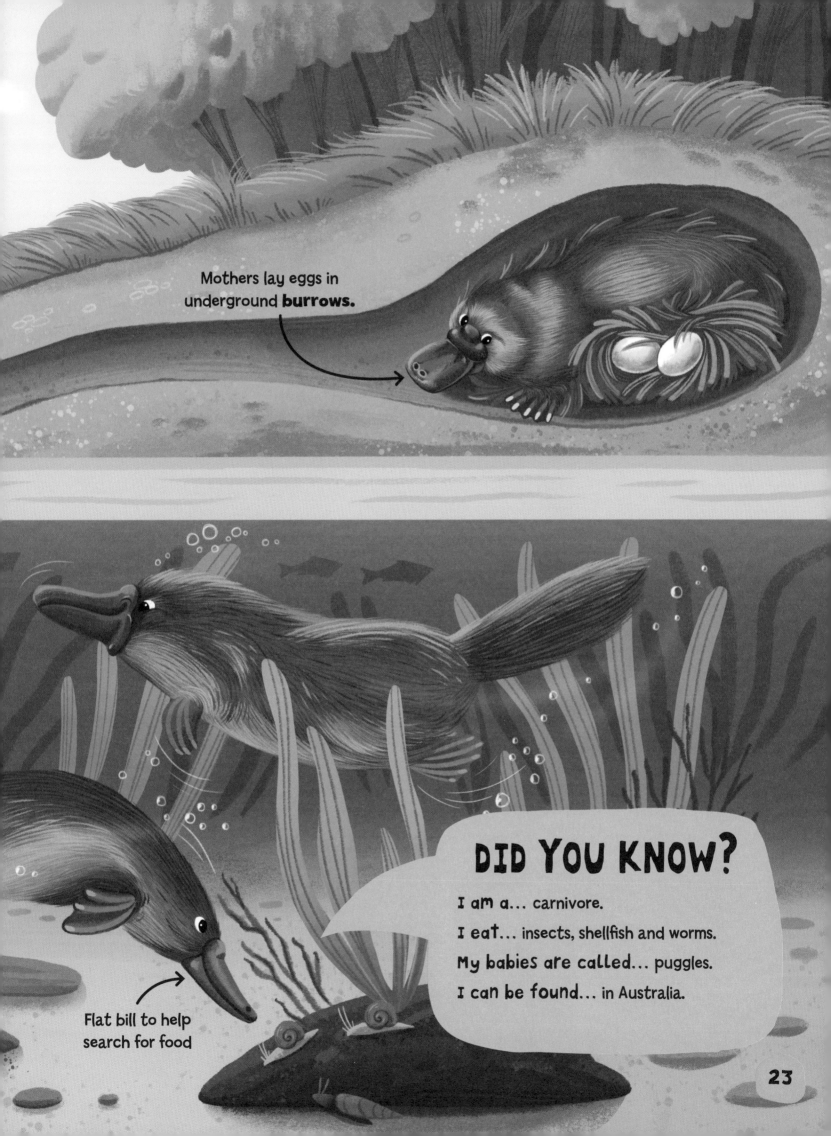

Mothers lay eggs in underground **burrows.**

Flat bill to help search for food

DID YOU KNOW?

I am a... carnivore.

I eat... insects, shellfish and worms.

My babies are called... puggles.

I can be found... in Australia.

SHEEP

Sheep are SUPER GRAZERS!

They are very gentle animals that live in groups called flocks and follow each other everywhere. Farmers often keep sheep on their farms to produce meat, milk and wool.

Strong horns used for wrestling

Male sheep are called rams.

Newborn lambs drink milk from their mother's udders.

Thick coat for keeping warm

DID YOU KNOW?

I am a... herbivore.

I eat... grass, plants and hay.

My babies are called... lambs.

I can be found... in America, Europe and Asia.

MOOSE

Moose are the LARGEST animals in the deer family!

Male moose have very impressive, strong antlers. They drop off every winter, then grow back again during spring! Although moose are big and heavy, these powerful giants are excellent swimmers.

Antlers for protecting themselves

Hooves help them travel on difficult ground.

DID YOU KNOW?

I am a... herbivore.

I eat... leaves, twigs and plants.

My babies are called... calves.

I can be found... in America, Canada, Europe and Asia.

Calves can outrun a human by the time they are 5 days old!

CHIMPANZEE

chimpanzees are very CLEVER ANIMALS!

Chimpanzees live in large groups called communities, led by the strongest male among them. They travel together and are often seen grooming each other too, showing they are close family and friends.

Long arms for swinging and climbing

They have **opposable thumbs.**

DID YOU KNOW?

I am an... omnivore.

I eat... fruit, nuts and insects.

My babies are called... infants.

I can be found... in Africa.

They use tools to feed and defend themselves.

CAMEL

camels have large HUMPS on their backs!

Camels can survive for long periods of time without drinking water because they don't sweat like humans do! That's very handy in their **desert** homes, where water is hard to find.

Camels store fat in their humps.

Three sets of eyelids protect their eyes during sandstorms.

They can also shut their nostrils!

DID YOU KNOW?

I am a... herbivore.

I eat... grass, leaves and twigs.

My babies are called... calves.

I can be found... in deserts around the world.

ARMADILLO

Armadillos are the only mammals that have HARD SHELLS!

They are one of the only species that can roll into a ball! They are **nocturnal** and spend up to 16 hours a day sleeping in their burrows.

Great sense of smell for hunting food

Protective shell to fend off predators

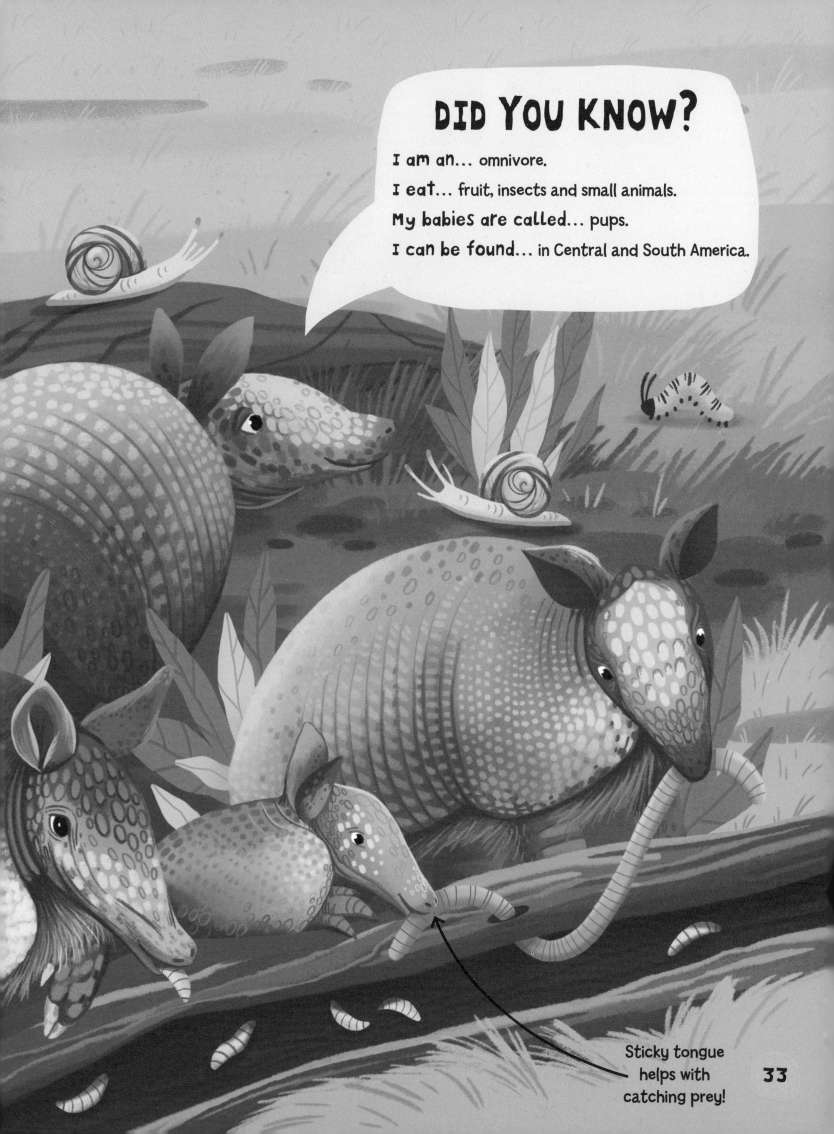

DID YOU KNOW?

I am an... omnivore.

I eat... fruit, insects and small animals.

My babies are called... pups.

I can be found... in Central and South America.

Sticky tongue helps with catching prey!

33

BAT

Bats are the only mammals in the world that can FLY!

Bats are nocturnal animals and sleep upside down so they can fly away quickly from predators. Bats are very sociable animals and live in big groups called colonies.

Sharp toe claws for grip

Big ears to find prey at night using **echolocation.**

DID YOU KNOW?

I am an... omnivore.

I eat... fruit, insects and small rodents.

My babies are called... pups.

I can be found... almost everywhere!

Thin wings make flying easy.

KANGAROO

A kangaroo can leap up to 30 feet (9 m) in the air WITH ONE BOUNCE!

Kangaroos live together in groups called troops. Male kangaroos fight using their own style of boxing to decide who the leader is.

DID YOU KNOW?

I am a... herbivore.

I eat... leaves and grass.

My babies are called... joeys.

I can be found... in Australia.

Females have a pouch where newborn joeys grow.

Powerful
back legs

Long tail
for balance

ELEPHANT

Elephants are the
HEAVIEST LAND MAMMALS!

An elephant can weigh up to 15,000 pounds (7,000kg)! They live in groups called herds that are led by female elephants. Elephants are very sociable and create strong family bonds with each other that last a lifetime.

Calves hold onto their mother's tail to stay safe.

Long trunk for smelling, drinking and picking up food

The **tusks** are actually huge teeth that stick out of an elephant's mouth.

Large ears help them stay cool.

DID YOU KNOW?

I am a... herbivore.

I eat... fruit, leaves and roots.

My babies are called... calves.

I can be found... in Africa and Asia.

DID YOU KNOW?

How many types of mammals are there?

Lots! There are around 6,000 different types of mammals in the world, but none are as tall as me!

What was the first mammal?

The first mammal was called Morganucodon (mor-gan-uh-cuh-don), and was a shrew-like animal, like me! It lived alongside the dinosaurs!

40

What is the most intelligent mammal?

Humans are the smartest mammals, but chimpanzees and whales are very clever too.

What is the quickest mammal?

A cheetah is the quickest mammal and can run up to 70 mph (113 km)! That's much faster than me!

NAME THAT MAMMAL

Can you work out which mammal each of these pictures are a part of?
Clues have been provided for you based on facts from this book!

CLUE: This mammal has antlers which it uses to protect itself.

CLUE: This mammal lives in the Arctic.

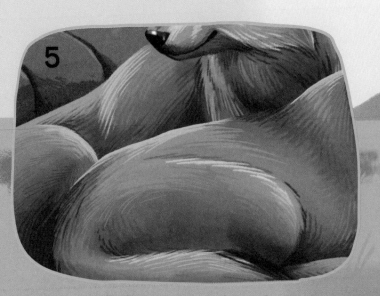

CLUE: This mammal can fly.

CLUE: This mammal hunts in groups called packs.

CLUE: This mammal has a hard shell.

CLUE: This mammal is the only mammal that can lay eggs.

CLUE: This mammal is the largest mammal in the world.

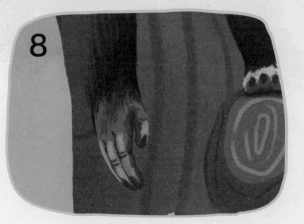

CLUE: This mammal has opposable thumbs.

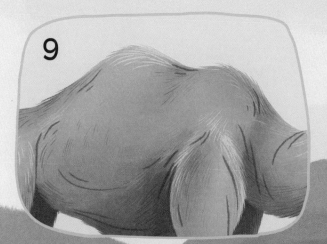

CLUE: This mammal has humps on its back to help store fat.

CLUE: This mammal can leap 30 feet (9 m) in the air with one bounce!

DID YOU FIND THEM ALL?

Answers can be found on page 44.

INDEX

First published in 2024 by Hungry Tomato Ltd.
F15, Old Bakery Studios, Blewetts Wharf,
Malpas Road, Truro, Cornwall, TR1 1QH, UK.

Thanks to our creative team:
Editor: Millie Burdett
Editor: Holly Thornton
Senior Designer: Amy Harvey

Copyright © 2024 Hungry Tomato Ltd

Beetle Books is an imprint of Hungry Tomato.

A CIP catalog record for this book is available from
the British Library.

ISBN: 9781915461940

Printed and bound in China

Discover more at
www.hungrytomato.com
www.mybeetlebooks.com

Match the Mammals Answers:

1 - Moose, 2 - Polar bear, 3 - Bat,
4 - Armadillo, 5 - Wolf, 6 - Platypus,
7 - Blue whale, 8 - Chimpanzee,
9 - Camel, 10 - Kangaroo.

GLOSSARY

Burrows – a tunnel dug by an animal in which they live, often underground.

Carnivore – an animal that mostly eats meat.

Desert – a place where it hardly ever rains.

Fungi – a group of living things that are neither plants or animals.

Echolocation – when animals use echoes from sound waves to move through their environment.

Grazing – to feed on growing grass.

Herbivore – an animal that only eats plants.

Nocturnal – an animal that sleeps during the day but becomes active during the night.

Omnivore – an animal that eats plants and meat, just like humans.

Opposable thumbs – thumbs that can move freely and independently (humans have them!).

Predators – animals that hunt and kill other animals for food.

Prey – animals which are hunted by other animals as food.

Tusks – long, sharp pointed teeth.

Venomous – animals that can produce poison in their body, allowing them to harm or kill other animals.